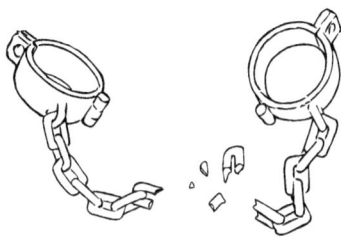

WORLDVIEW GUIDE

NARRATIVE OF THE LIFE
OF FREDERICK DOUGLASS

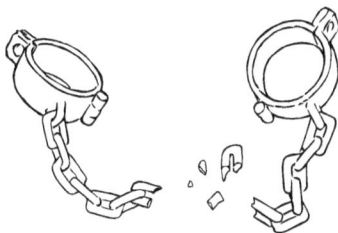

Jake Meador

canonpress
Moscow, Idaho

Published by Canon Press
P.O. Box 8729, Moscow, Idaho 83843
800.488.2034 | www.canonpress.com

Jake Meador, *Worldview Guide for Narrative of the Life of Frederick Douglass*
Copyright © 2018 by Jake Meador.
For the Canon Classics edition of the novel go to www.canonpress.com/books/
canon-classics.

Cover design by James Engerbretson
Cover illustration by Forrest Dickison
Interior design by Valerie Anne Bost and James Engerbretson

Printed in the United States of America.

Scripture quotations are from the Authorized Version.

Library of Congress Cataloging-in-Publication Data
Meador, Jake, author.
Worldview guide : Narrative of the life of Frederick Douglass, an
   American slave / Jake Meador.
Moscow, Idaho : Canon Press, [2019]
LCCN 2018056798 | ISBN 9781947644311 (pbk. : alk. paper)
LCSH: Douglass, Frederick, 1818-1895. Narrative of the life of
   Frederick Douglass, an American slave. | Douglass, Frederick,
   1818-1895—Religion. | Slave narratives—History and criticism. |
   Slavery—Religious aspects—Christianity. | Slavery—United
   States—History—19th century. | Southern States—Religion. |
   Slaves—United States—Biography.
Classification: LCC E449 .M478 2019 | DDC 973.8092—dc23
LC record available at https://lccn.loc.gov/2018056798

A free end-of-book test and answer key are available for download at
www.canonpress.com/ClassicsQuizzes

18 19 20 21 22 23   9 8 7 6 5 4 3 2 1

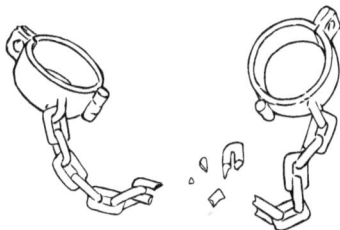

CONTENTS

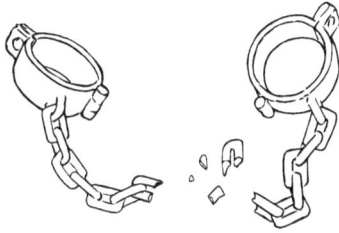

INTRODUCTION

There's an interesting moment in 2 Kings 18:4 that can easily pass you by. It says, "[King Hezekiah] removed the high places, and brake the images, and cut down the groves, and brake in pieces the brasen serpent that Moses had made: for unto those days the children of Israel did burn incense to it: and he called it Nehushtan." The serpent in the text refers to the incident in the book of Numbers when the Israelites are attacked by poisonous snakes as a judgment from God for their repeated unfaithfulness. God directs Moses to fashion a serpent from bronze and hoist it up above the camp. Any Israelites who looked toward the bronze serpent would be saved. Though the serpent became an idol several hundred years later, it is striking that we find God's people keeping for many, many years something that would have reminded them of their failures.

In a day when most anything can be rendered disposable, Americans are not accustomed to keeping things that remind them of times of darkness, sadness, or failure. We do not keep the nameplate from the job where we were fired. We do not keep the bad report card or the paper that got an F. It is common for divorced couples to "purge" their homes of things that remind them of their former husband or wife. Nationally, we do not build monuments to commemorate our nation's greatest failures. There is no Richard Nixon Memorial in Washington, nor is there a pillar to commemorate the Great Depression erected anywhere near Wall Street, though one can't help wondering if things might have played out differently in 2008 if there were. In America we forget the bad and try to remember the positive. We are the consummate optimists.

This idea of a negative memorial, something we keep that serves as a warning to us of the dire consequences of falling into sin, is perhaps a useful starting place for considering Frederick Douglass's remarkable *Narrative*. If we are to understand both the good and the bad in America, there may be no better text to begin with than with this book.

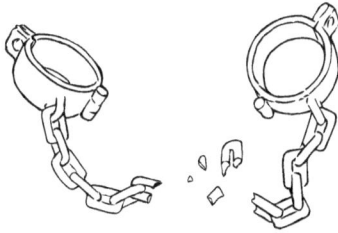

THE WORLD AROUND

Douglass was born sometime in February of 1818 in Maryland. At the time Maryland was a slave state, but its northern border was part of the old Mason-Dixon line that divided free states from slave states. Often this meant that slavery in Maryland was not as brutal as slavery in states further south, such as Alabama or Mississippi. These things are relative, of course, because slavery in Maryland was still exceedingly brutal.

In terms of the broader historical moment, at the time of his birth James Monroe was in the White House. John Adams, Thomas Jefferson, and James Madison were still living and Abraham Lincoln was a nine-year-old boy living in Illinois. Many of the most difficult legal battles regarding slavery were still yet to come. The nation was still in its infancy at this point, and there were a number of questions that, at Douglass's birth, were still unanswered—such as the legal status of an escaped slave living in the North or even the basic ability of non-white people to own property. These questions would be legally resolved during Douglass's early life.

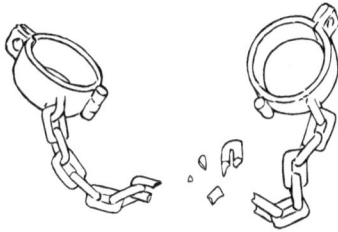

ABOUT THE AUTHOR

Frederick Douglass was born a slave in Maryland and escaped to freedom after teaching himself to read as a young man. After arriving in the North, he quickly became involved in abolitionist work alongside white abolitionists like William Lloyd Garrison, publisher of *The Liberator*. Douglass's giftedness as a communicator and speaker became quickly apparent to his new friends and he soon began speaking publicly for the cause of abolition.

The Narrative of the Life of Frederick Douglass is notable for a number of reasons. First, the sheer forcefulness of the man's prose made the book impossible to ignore. Douglass was a remarkable communicator and orator. His ability to tell the truth about American slavery is perhaps unparalleled amongst antebellum writers. Second, Douglass went on to a very successful career after the Civil War and was one of the first African Americans to hold a number of major governmental positions, working as a US Marshall for the District of Columbia and later serving as an ambassador to Haiti. Both in terms of his talent as a writer and his professional success, it is hard to find many who can rival Douglass.

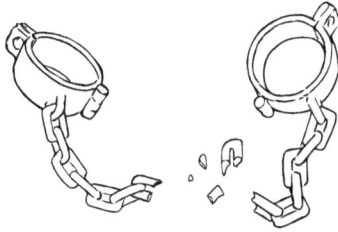

WHAT OTHER
NOTABLES SAID

Garrison and Douglass were close friends for a decade. When he first heard Douglass speak, Garrison turned to the crowd after Douglass finished and asked, "Have we been listening to the testimony of a piece of property or a man?" When the crowd shouted back "a man!" he asked, "Can we ever allow such a man to be treated as property?" "Never!" said the crowd. "Can you doubt that such treatment is the grossest sin?" The crowd said "No!" Finally, he asked them, "Then will you pledge with us to end this sin and crime in which three million of our fellow beings are not seen as fellow citizens, but simply as property and tools of another to use as he will?"[1]

---

1. Michael Westmoreland-White, "Garrison and Douglass: Friendship and Estrangement," https://pilgrimpathways.wordpress.com/2010/07/29/garrison-and-douglass-friendship-and-estrangement/, accessed August 25, 2017.

Douglass would meet President Lincoln in August of 1863 to discuss his work recruiting black men to serve in the Union army. They had a somewhat heated meeting, as Douglass pushed the president to guarantee equal pay for black soldiers and to take actions to recognize black soldiers for meritorious conduct in battles. The president repeatedly affirmed Douglass's long-term desires, but said that getting to his objectives would take more time. Though the meeting was, at times, tense, Douglass came away from it saying that he was "not entirely satisfied (by the president's views)," but that he was, "so well satisfied with the man…that I determined to go on with the recruiting."[2]

---

2. Rick Beard, "When Douglass Met Lincoln," *The New York Times*, August 9, 2013, accessed August 25, 2017.

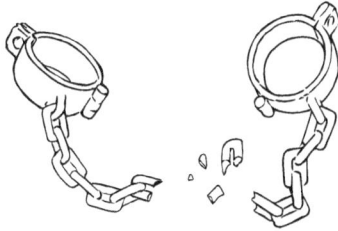

PLOT SUMMARY, SETTING, AND CHARACTERS

Much of the book's action takes place in antebellum Maryland. Douglass worked in both the house and on the farm, so he is able to describe what both looked like on a day-to-day basis for a normal slave.

Frederick Douglass was born at a time when several of the men who had signed the Declaration of Independence, which said that all men are created equal, were still alive. The facts of Douglass's life are a stark refutation of Jefferson's words. Indeed, the fact of Douglass's conception is itself a refutation of those words as Douglass was the child of his master and one of his master's slaves. Rape was an inescapable aspect of the brutality of slavery.

All across the Western Hemisphere, beginning in the forests of Brazil and working its way as far north as Douglass's Maryland, European Christians enforced a horrifying regime on black human beings made in the image of God. In one particularly chilling account, we learn that the manager of a plantation in the Caribbean flogged a slave and then "pickled him" by rubbing salt pickle, lime juice, and bird pepper into the fresh wounds of the slave. Then, he had another slave defecate in the slave's mouth.

To be sure, some places were more brutal than others—Douglass's Maryland never approaches what was common in Central America for the simple reason that Maryland's close proximity to the Northern states had a chastening effect on the state's slaveowners. Even so, Douglass's life was still often quite horrifying. To take one famous example, Douglass describes how slave children were not given sufficient clothing to stay warm during the winter. They were given a single burlap sack and, when it came time to sleep, they had to decide if they would rather their head or their feet be exposed. Douglass chose to leave his feet uncovered and suffered severe frostbite as a result. As he wrote his narrative in the early 1840s, he said that "my feet have been so cracked with the frost, that the pen with which I am writing might be laid in the gashes" (22-23).

There are other examples you will encounter in the text as well. For instance, the most horrifying of the punishments Douglass recounts is the experience of a woman named Henny:

> I have seen him [Douglass's master] tie up a lame
> young woman, and whip her with a heavy cousin
> [whip] upon her naked shoulders, causing the warm
> red blood to drip; and, in justification of the bloody

deed, he would quote this passage of Scripture—
'He that knoweth his master's will, and doth it not,
shall be beaten with many stripes.' Master would
keep this lacerated young woman tied up in this
horrid situation four or five hours at a time. I have
known him to tie her up early in the morning, and
whip her before breakfast; leave her, go to his store,
return at dinner, and whip her again, cutting her
in the places already made raw with his cruel lash.
(47-48)[3]

Douglass's unflinching portrayal of American slavery
is horrifying, but the horror is precisely the point: We
should never forget exactly *how* bad and ugly and terrifying this institution was, nor should we forget how will-
ing Americans were to tolerate this institution. Indeed, as
we consider that last point we should become even more
discomforted.

---

3. All pages numbers taken from the Canon Classics edition (2016).

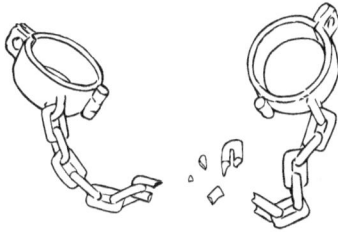

WORLDVIEW ANALYSIS

One point Douglass returns to over and over in his narrative is the religiosity of many slaveholders. Douglass's master, who was renowned for his religiosity, could quote Scripture while he beat his crippled slave and could do so not only without remorse, but firm in his belief that he was actually doing what the Scriptures taught. How are we to make sense of this?

The first extended discussion of Southern religion in Douglass's work comes early in the book as he discusses the effect that his master's conversion experience had on his treatment of his slaves. Simply put, his master was more brutal after his religious experience—which I am reluctant to call a conversion—than he was before. Douglass had his theory as to why this was: "Prior to his conversion, he relied upon his own depravity to shield and sustain him in his savage barbarity; but after his conversion, he found religious sanction and support for his slave-holding cruelty" (46).

Put another way, Douglass believed his master was aware of the evil of his behavior prior to his conversion, but his depravity insulated him from the full judgment of his own conscience. After his conversion, however, he acquired a religious justification for his slavery that emboldened him because it caused him to believe that he was acting righteously in his treatment of his slaves.

Douglass's description of Mr. Covey is similar: His neighbors all believed him to be "a pious soul" and he himself professed Christian faith and taught Sunday School at his local Methodist church. Yet this did nothing to alter Covey's treatment of his slaves. He forced them to work in all weather and was particularly known for hiding out near the fields where the slaves worked so that he could then unexpectedly spring out of the bushes to beat any slaves failing to work hard enough.

So how did Douglass make sense of this religion he saw in the antebellum South? He addresses the question directly at the end of the *Narrative*. The answer will be familiar to readers of the Gospels: He says that the religion of the slaveholders is not true religion, but is rather the religion of the Pharisees, of those people who tithe from their spice racks while failing to attend to the most basic demands of religious life. Douglass's summary of this religion is withering, but no more severe than the words of Christ to the Pharisees or those of the prophets to Israel:

> I am filled with unutterable loathing when I
> contemplate the religious pomp and show, togeth-
> er with the horrible inconsistencies, which every
> where surround me. We have men-stealers for min-
> isters, women-whippers for missionaries, and cra-
> dle-plunderers for church members. The man who
> wields the blood-clotted cousin [a whip] during the
> week fills the pulpit on Sunday, and claims to be a
> minister of the meek and lowly Jesus. The man who
> robs me of my earnings at the end of each week
> meets me as a class-leader on Sunday morning, to
> show me the way of life, and the path of salvation.
> He who sells my sister, for purposes of prostitution,
> stands forth as the pious advocate of purity. He
> who proclaims it a religious duty to read the Bible
> denies me the right of learning to read the name of
> the God who made me. He who is the religious ad-
> vocate of marriage robs whole millions of its sacred
> influence, and leaves them to the ravages of whole-
> sale pollution. The warm defender of the sacredness
> of the family relation is the same that scatters whole
> families,—sundering husbands and wives, parents
> and children, sisters and brothers,—leaving the hut
> vacant, and the hearth desolate. (97-98)

There are two things worth noting in this devastating denunciation of Southern religion. First, it is worth noting how *biblical* this language actually is. Throughout the Old Testament prophets we find writers inspired by God saying many of the same things to God's people, noting how their attendance to the external rituals of religion means nothing when it is divorced from a transformed life. In

Amos 5:21-23, God says to Israel, "I hate, I despise your feast days, and I will not smell in your solemn assemblies. Though ye offer me burnt offerings and your meat offerings, I will not accept them: neither will I regard the peace offerings of your fat beasts. Take thou away from me the noise of thy songs; for I will not hear the melody of thy viols." (The verse immediately following this denunciation of Israel, Amos 5:24, was famously quoted in Martin Luther King Jr's "I have a Dream" Speech.)

Jesus, of course, speaks in these terms throughout the Gospels. Jesus condemns the Pharisees with these words,

> Woe unto you, scribes and Pharisees, hypocrites,
> for ye pay the tithe of mint and anise and cummin,
> and have omitted the weightier matters of the law,
> judgment, mercy, and faith: these ought ye to have
> done, and not to leave the other undone. Ye blind
> guides, which strain at a gnat, and swallow a camel.
> Woe unto you, scribes and Pharisees, hypocrites,
> for ye make clean the outside of the cup and of the
> platter, but within they are full of extortion and
> excess. (Matt. 23:23-25)

Douglass is not making any of these criticisms as someone outside of the Church. Nowhere in the *Narrative* does Douglass repudiate Christianity itself. Rather, Douglass himself is a Christian and this is precisely why he is as aggressive as he is in his denunciation of white Southern Christianity. It is his love of Christ that drives his fierce rhetoric:

> For, between the Christianity of this land, and
> the Christianity of Christ, I recognize the widest
> possible difference—so wide, that to receive the
> one as good, pure, and holy, is of necessity to reject
> the other as bad, corrupt, and wicked. To be the
> friend of the one, is of necessity to be the enemy of
> the other. I love the pure, peaceable, and impartial
> Christianity of Christ: I therefore hate the corrupt,
> slave-holding, women-whipping, cradle-plundering,
> partial and hypocritical Christianity of this land."

And take note of how Douglass closes this salvo,

> "Indeed, I can see no reason, but the most deceitful
> one, for calling the religion of this land Christianity.
> I look upon it as the climax of all misnomers, the
> boldest of all frauds, and the grossest of all libels.
> (97)

This, then, is the final lesson we must learn about how to read Douglass's *Narrative* as a kind of negative memorial to the American Idea and to American Christianity.

You Must Love Pimlico

In his essay "The Flag of the World" published in *Orthodoxy*, G. K. Chesterton argues that the only way to transform a desperate and blighted thing is to love it. In one place, he defends loving Pimlico, a section of London:

> It is not enough for a man to disapprove of Pimlico:
> in that case he will merely cut his throat or move to
> [another neighborhood]. Nor, certainly, is it enough

for a man to approve of Pimlico: for then it will re-
main Pimlico, which would be awful. The only way
out of it seems to be for somebody to love Pimlico:
to love it with a transcendental tie and without
any earthly reason. If there arose a man who loved
Pimlico, then Pimlico would rise into ivory towers
and golden pinnacles; Pimlico would attire herself
as a woman does when she is loved.[4]

This is what must be kept in mind as we read Douglass's *Narrative*. It is striking that Douglass's fiery de-
nunciations of the American Church are fueled not by
seeing himself as an outsider, but by seeing himself as a
fellow member of that religion. It is precisely his love for
Christ that drives him to condemn the cruelty of American Christians. This is an important point because it is
only this sort of love that can truly address the sort of social problems that Douglass's *Narrative* describes in such
unflinching language. Fierce moral condemnation and patriotism do not exist in competition with one another, but
alongside one another.

Far too often, people read American history in one
of two ways. Progressives spend too much time reading
Howard Zinn and James Loewen and come to see America as one of the greatest evils ever to exist on earth. Every
notable act in American history, even ones that seem to be
rather unambiguously good, must be cynically interpreted
in such a way as to preserve the America-is-bad narrative

---

4. *Orthodoxy* (New York: John Lane, 1908), 122.

to which this side has given itself. And so those who read American history in this way become like the sort of boor that we all know and none of us like, the sort of person who is a constant grumbler and complainer, who is never content and can never offer praise or commendation removed from criticisms offered in greater measure. These are the sort of people who have come to hate what has been given to them but who lack any capacity for love that might help them escape or improve what has been given.

Conservatives, however, frequently engage in the opposite error. We publish texts like the *American Patriot's Bible* and whitewash American history to remove all the nasty bits and uncomfortable facts. At worst, we become like David Barton, a man so determined to sanitize all of American history that he would transform Thomas Jefferson, the famed deist who quite literally used a razor blade to remove the supernatural parts of the Gospels from his Bible, into an orthodox evangelical Christian. For these people there is no need to work for America's improvement because America has already been perfected. The only work to be done is the polemical work of disputing those people who fail to understand that fact and the legislative work needed to protect that perfection.

In both cases, these readers of American history are left radically unequipped and unprepared to live as responsible members of the American republic. If we are going to love our home, we have to be able to see it for what it is and, despite what we see, continue to love it and, because of that love, work for its health, peace, and prosperity. And we must be clear on exactly how bad what we see is likely going to be. We are, after all, dealing with a republic made up of sinful human beings and in which certain sins have become particularly entrenched over many centuries. We should not pass over this point glibly. What we find when we look at our republic will routinely be horrifying. That said, the horror and the hope exist alongside one another because we are Christian people who know that we worship a God who has conquered sin and death. We are, therefore, able to look at the world as it really is and still, despite that, hope for its transformation and work to bring that about through a life of love.

Those on the left inclined to see America only as a demon would do well to consider how miraculous the founding of our republic truly was and how unique and life-giving the American Idea has been for many ordinary people in our country who, thanks to our experiment in self-government, were emancipated from centuries-old systems that governed small, local places from afar and placed heavy burdens on the backs of ordinary people. This part of America really does exist and is worth loving.

But those on the right who see America only as angel would do equally well to attend closely to texts like Douglass's *Narrative*. The same founders who established such a remarkable republic chose to look the other way when the issue of slavery arose. Their failure on this point is responsible for the sufferings of famous slaves like Douglass and of the forgotten slaves like Henny. Moreover, the American commitment to slavery is uniquely strong and horrifying even amongst that of other Western nations that tolerated chattel slavery. Unlike their more admirable peers in the United Kingdom, 19th century Americans proved incapable of eliminating slavery through any means save that of a brutal and bloody civil war. And even after we eliminated slavery, we only replaced it with sharecropping, Jim Crow, lynching, and, more contemporarily, mass incarceration.

The human suffering created by American slavery specifically and American racism more generally is a galling and terrifying thing. If you would be a patriot, if you would be someone well fit to belong to this republic and to work for its good, you must understand that fact. And you must understand that the same evil that allowed 19th-century Americans to tolerate such a terror exists within our own hearts today. If we would be saved from committing sins that are no less horrifying than those of Mr. Covey, we must repent and follow the Christ that this book's author loved so fiercely.

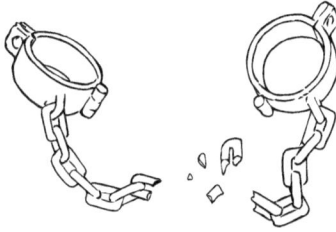

QUOTABLES

1. "I have often been utterly astonished, since I came to the north, to find persons who could speak of the singing, among slaves, as evidence of their contentment and happiness. It is impossible to conceive of a greater mistake. Slaves sing most when they are most unhappy. The songs of the slave represent the sorrows of his heart; and he is relieved by them, only as an aching heart is relieved by its tears.... The singing of a man cast away upon a desolate island might be as appropriately considered as evidence of contentment and happiness...." (12)

2. "Freedom now appeared, to disappear no more forever. It was heard in every sound and seen in every thing. It was very present to torment me with a sense of my wretched condition. I saw nothing without seeing it, I heard nothing without hearing it, and felt nothing without feeling it. It looked from every star, it smiled in

every calm, breathed in every wind, and moved in every storm." (34)

3. "The argument which [my master] so warmly urged, against my learning to read, only served to inspire me with a desire and a determination to learn. In learning to read, I owe almost as much to the bitter opposition of my master, as to the kindly aid of my mistress. I acknowledge the benefit of both." (29)

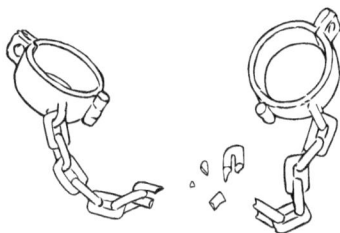

21 SIGNIFICANT QUESTIONS AND ANSWERS

1. What are some biblical examples of a negative memorial?

   In terms of physical artifacts, the obvious example is the bronze serpent which we mentioned previously. Paul also seems to see the history of God's people in the Old Testament as a kind of negative memorial, which is why he argues the way that he does in 1 Cor. 10.

2. How can negative memorials help God's people avoid sin?

   Negative memorials function basically the same way that positive memorials do: They remind us of something that it would be bad for us to forget. The difference is that they are reminding us of something we should not do again. But in most ways, they

function as any other memorial would: Remember
this because this historical fact should change the
way you act.

3. What key moment in his early life gives Douglass hope
that he can escape slavery?

> The most important thing that happens is Douglass
> learning to read. By learning to read, he is able to
> imagine a way to freedom because he is able to see
> himself as something other than a slave.

4. How do his owners deal with Douglass after this? Do
they succeed in breaking his spirit?

> Douglass's owners send him to a man renowned for
> being a "slave breaker." Douglass endures several
> hard beatings from the man before one day when
> he is taken aside for a beating and he decides to
> fight back. And then something happens that
> Douglass did not expect: He survives. The slave
> breaker, it turned out, did not want the story getting
> out that he had been beaten by a slave.

5. How were these two incidents key to Douglass's
emancipation, not only from the physical condition of
slavery, but from the mentality of the slave?

> Through reading, Douglass realized that he was
> intelligent enough not only to learn to read, but also
> to live on his own outside of the slave system. He
> developed the inner strength that he would come to

believe is essential to breaking out of an institution like Southern slavery. When he fought back against the slave breaker, Douglass realized that he is not simply a passive receptacle for white cruelty. Even in his state as a piece of property, he still possessed his humanity and, with it, real agency.

6. How do the white slaveowners justify their treatment of their slaves?

The underlying belief that upheld slavery is the idea that different races had different capabilities and "proper" roles within a social hierarchy. This was a common view across the South and actually could be found in the North as well in a modified, less overt form. You can find it in evangelicals writing about the issue, such as the Southern Presbyterian R. L. Dabney.

Because it was widely believed that Africans were innately inferior to whites, it was held that slavery was a good status for them and that slaves who aspired to something higher actually were going against nature and, as such, were actually doing harm to themselves. This, in turn, could justify the treatment of slaves that Douglass describes.

7. What effect does slavery have on the slaveowners according to Douglass?

Douglass observed that once a person became comfortable with slavery, they became capable of cruelty that would have seemed strange and horrifying to them prior to encountering slavery. Slavery creates a strange kind of space in the mind in which things that would horrify a normal human being can be justified as being okay.

8. How should the antebellum slaveowners have dealt with slavery?

There are a couple different answers to this question. The obvious and conclusive answer is through repentance—submitting themselves to Christ and treating human beings as people made in the image of God and, therefore, possessing a certain nobility and deserving of respect. That said, political structures and systems push people towards certain ends. A society that tolerates abortion, for example, leads to a number of people who view unborn children as being somehow less *really* human than babies who have already been born. Slavery works in a similar way. It creates a political structure that legitimizes the abuse of a large group of people. So there is also a strong argument to be made that the answer to this question is "abolition." Abolition would not have solved all the problems with slavery in a final, conclusive way. But it would have removed the structures that shape people in certain ways. Just as we would not say that we shouldn't end abortion because that won't save the abortion doctors, in the same way just because preaching the gospel to slaveowners was necessary did not also take away the need for political reform.

9. What role did Christianity play in the lives of the slaveowners?

> For Christians, slavery wasn't simply an econom-
> ic system. It was actually the best possible social
> system for the slaves themselves because they were
> thought to be incapable of governing themselves
> and so they were incapable of any way of life
> besides slavery. This gave a religious justification
> for slavery which took it from being simply an
> economic system that served the interests of white
> southerners to being a system of life endorsed by
> God.

10. What role did Christianity play in Douglass's life?

> What is striking when you read the *Narrative*
> is how Douglass uses the religion of the slavers
> against them. Christianity for Douglass is not
> synonymous with a white man's religion. Rather, it
> is something he also confesses, and it is precisely
> because of his commitment to it that he attacks the
> false religion of the slaveowners with such vehe-
> mence. Within the context of the *Narrative*, then,
> there is a sense in which Douglass's Christianity is
> a major source of the book's moral critique of the
> antebellum South.

11. What are the most common responses to slavery amongst the white people Douglass knows early in his life?

> There are two main reactions, neither of which are good. The first reaction is to essentially grimace a little and look away but not actually do anything to aid the slaves. This is an acknowledgement of the evil of slavery, but it is of no use because it is not followed by practical action. The other response is of the sort described by Wendell Berry in *The Hidden Wound*. Essentially, if you are a Christian *and* you participate in something as horrific as slavery, the only way you can do it for long is by essentially erecting a divide in your mind to justify the dissonance between your stated faith and your actual behavior. The atheist writer Christopher Hitchens once said that Dostoevsky had it wrong when he said that if God did not exist anything could be permitted. Hitchens said that actually it is only *with* God that anything can be permissible because if you discover a mandate from heaven you can justify the most horrific abuses of human beings.

12. Douglass is concerned not only with the physical condition of slavery, but also with what that condition does to a person's self-image. What are some of the ways that Douglass sees slavery shaping the way his fellow slaves see themselves?

> Under slavery and later under segregation you eventually become used to unjust treatment and begin

to believe that you deserve it. In the *Brown v. Board* case that ended *de jure* segregation of schools one of the main arguments made by Thurgood Marshall's team came from a study done by a black psychiatrist named Kenneth Clark. Clark interviewed hundreds of black school children in an attempt to measure how segregation affected their self-image. So he would sit down with school children and show them a black doll and a white doll and then ask them to do things with the dolls. "Show me the good doll," "Show me the bad doll," "Show me the doll that looks like you." By doing this, Clark established how even schoolchildren under a segregation system internalized an inferior view of themselves. This learned inferiority and the way in which it makes the person easier to exploit is a huge concern of Douglass's and is something he comes back to throughout his *Narrative*.

13. Why does Douglass say so little about his escape from slavery?

It is important to remember the book's history here. *The Narrative* was published in 1845, 16 years before the start of the Civil War. According to the 1840 census, there were 2,487,355 slaves in the United States at this time. So there were still nearly two and a half million people in the antebellum South living under slavery. Douglass would not want to do *anything* to hurt their chances of escape. So not explaining how he escaped is one part of that broader caution that defined his early years after escaping.

14. What role does trickery play in Douglass's develop-
ment as a person and his escape from slavery?

> The chief way we see trickery used is the use of the
> root offered to Douglass by Sandy Jenkins before
> his fateful encounter with Edward Covey, the slave
> breaker. The trick here isn't simply that the slave is
> now able to resist the slave-breaker. Going into the
> woods to receive a root from a black man would
> be seen as a hearkening to the herbal medicines of
> black slaves in the Caribbean and the deep south.
> It's a way of asserting the power of African medi-
> cine against the cruelty of the white man.

15. Was the north free of the underlying spirit that contrib-
uted to the cruelty of the antebellum south?

> There were many structural and cultural difficulties
> awaiting free blacks in the north. For example, the
> northern abolitionist David Walker, who lived in
> Boston, MA, wrote in his *Appeal*:

> "I ask those people who treat us so well, Oh! I ask
> them, where is the most barren spot of land which
> they have given unto us? Israel had the most fertile
> land in all Egypt. Need I mention the very notori-
> ous fact, that I have known a poor man of colour,
> who laboured night and day, to acquire a little mon-
> ey, and having acquired it, he vested it in a small
> piece of land, and got him a house erected thereon,
> and having paid for the whole, he moved his family
> into it, where he was suffered to remain but nine

months, when he was cheated out of his property
by a white man, and driven out of door! And is not
this the case generally? Can a man of colour buy a
piece of land and keep it peaceably? Will not some
white man try to get it from him, even if it is in a
mud hole? I need not comment any farther on a
subject, which all, both black and white, will readily
admit. But I must, really, observe that in this very
city, when a man of colour dies, if he owned any real
estate it most generally falls into the hands of some
white person. The wife and children of the deceased
may weep and lament if they please, but the estate
will be kept snug enough by its white possessor."[5]

Sadly, after Walker's death from tuberculosis this is
exactly what happened to his wife and children.

16. How does Douglass think about the United States as a
nation and the rights listed in the founding documents?

Douglass makes the argument that both the
American project itself and Christian faith, which
is often lumped in with America in many of these
works, are foundationally just and morally sound,
but the actual practice of individual people is what
is broken. Consequently, the response is to call
white American Christians to actually live up to

---

5. *Walker's Appeal, in Four Articles; Together with a Preamble to the Coloured Citizens of the World, but in Particular, and Very Expressly to Those of the United States of America* (1829).

the standards given by their own nation and the
teachings of their own religion.

17. Douglass, observing his mistress' change of heart, says
"Slavery proved as injurious to her as it did to me."
Why did Mrs. Auld change her treatment of Frederick
Douglass?

> Slavery does not just hurt Douglass. It hurts Mrs.
> Auld by teaching her that it is legitimate to hate
> people made in God's image. Specifically, it first
> teaches her that it is permissable to abuse and
> treat those people violently. But this also, over
> time, amounts to a tacit assent to hatred more
> generally. If it is lawful to beat this human being,
> then is it not lawful to hate them?

18. What are some other moments in history that we as
Americans should be ashamed of?

> The most clear-cut moments of national moral
> tragedy are slavery and abortion, both of which
> have been responsible for the death of untold
> masses and have impacted the lives of millions
> more. Other places where we can see it include
> the broader history of racism in the United States,
> the genocide of the Native American popula-
> tion, harsh immigration policies like the Chinese
> Exclusion Act, and continued forms of legal and
> de facto injustice against African Americans in-
> cluding, but not limited to, lynching, segregation,
> medical experimentation, and mass incarceration.
> At bottom, all of these grievous sins fail to reckon

with the fact that human beings—all human beings—are made in the image and likeness of God.

19. Why do people ignore gross injustices in their society?

There seem to be two main ways we can ignore
injustice. The first way is to try to block out the recognition of it because confronting it would be too
painful. A friend of mine once said that often the
most cynical people are also the most idealistic—
cynicism is simply a way of dealing with the sharp
pain they feel when their ideals are not realized.
The second way to ignore injustice is to lose oneself
in a labyrinth of material comfort and superficial
relationships.

20. What should we do about injustices in our society that we seem to be unable to defeat?

This is a difficult question. On the one hand,
there is a real sense in which it is appropriate to
acknowledge our limitations as human beings,
trust that God is good, and limit how much news
we consume. On the other, this wise recognition of
our finiteness can easily become a sinful indiffer-
ence to the sufferings of our fellow human beings.
Here we would do well to remember that while
we are not called to achieve the redemption of
all things—that is Christ's job, after all—we are
called to follow Him in the place where He has
put us and to work for the good of our neighbors
in that place. This world is the theatre of God, a

realm in which we will never meet a mere mortal. That homeless man you see on the street will one day be a beauty so great you'd be tempted to worship or a horror so perverted that you would have to look away upon seeing him (cf. C.S. Lewis's *The Weight of Glory*). What he is not, what he can never be, is an insignificant person, a person you can glibly walk past on the street or dismiss as self-evidently a lazy bum, completely responsible for whatever straits he has fallen into.

21. Why was slavery in the city less barbaric than the slavery out on plantations?

> States closer to the North, like Douglass's Maryland, tended to be less cruel than states in the deep south. This is because news of especially brutal treatment of slaves was more likely to reach the North—and the newspapers—if the treatment happened in Baltimore, where northerners often visited. If it happened in rural Alabama, then odds were quite good that no one outside of the plantation would ever become aware of it, save perhaps slave traders and people they choose to tell about it. Similarly, cities and the plantation house itself were also more public than rural areas or the fields themselves.

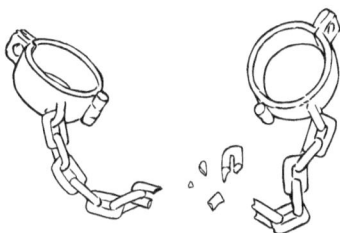

FURTHER DISCUSSION AND REVIEW

Master what you have read by reviewing and integrating the different elements of this classic.

AUTHOR AND SETTING

Be able to describe the life and career of Frederick Douglass. Also, be able to summarize how that relates to his principles, and explain whether that makes you respect him more or not.

PLOT

Be able to describe the beginning, middle, and end of the book along with the major teachings of the book. This includes both things that you agree and disagree with. Explain what makes this book compelling.

PHILOSOPHICAL ISSUES

Be able to describe what this classic is telling us about the world. Is the message true? What truth can we take from the argument and philosophical questions discussed? What kind of influence has Frederick Douglass had on history? Finally, be able to interact with the following philosophical and practical questions (or any others you've noticed) from this classic:

- What is true patriotism?
- How do we deal with corporate sins in our nation's past?
- How do people justify hypocrisy?
- How can even religious people justify cruelty?
- How do we deal with injustices in our society?
- What are basic human rights? What is freedom?

Finally, identify another issue, large or small, in this classic. Use the Bible and common sense to evaluate Frederick Douglass's approach to that issue. If you need it, you can use the list of key issues on pages 13–14 as a starting point.

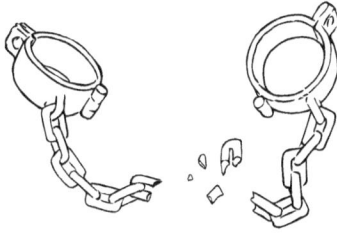

A NOTE FROM THE PUBLISHER:
TAKING THE CLASSICS QUIZ

Once you have finished the worldview guide, you can prepare for the end-of-book test. Each test will consist of a short-answer section on the book itself and the author, a short-answer section on plot and the narrative, and a long-answer essay section on worldview, conflict, and themes.

Each quiz, along with other helps, can be downloaded for free at www.canonpress.com/ClassicsQuizzes. If you have any questions about the quiz or its answers or the Worldview Guides in general, you can contact Canon Press at service@canonpress.com or 208.892.8074.

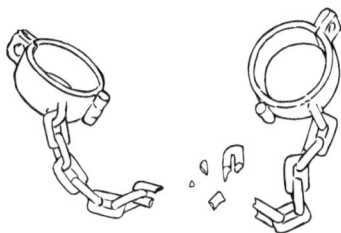

ABOUT THE AUTHOR

Jake Meador is a graduate of the University of Nebraska-Lincoln where he studied English and History. He lives in Lincoln, NE with his wife Joie, their daughter Davy Joy, and sons Wendell and Austin. Jake's writing has appeared in *Christianity Today*, *Fare Forward*, *The University Bookman*, *Books & Culture*, *First Things*, *Front Porch Republic*, and *The Run of Play*.

www.ingramcontent.com/pod-product-compliance
Lightning Source LLC
Chambersburg PA
CBHW071936020426
42331CB00010B/2901